Miscarriage

....

You Are Not Alone

Stephanie Green

New
Growth
Press

www.newgrowthpress.com

New Growth Press, Greensboro, NC 27404
www.newgrowthpress.com
Copyright © 2014 by Stephanie Green

All Scripture quotations, unless otherwise indicated, are taken
from the *New American Standard Bible,* © Copyright 1960, 1962,
1963, 1968, 1971, 1972, 1973, 1975, 1977, 1995 by The Lockman
Foundation. Used by permission.

Cover Design: Faceout Books, faceoutstudio.com
Typesetting: Lisa Parnell, Thompson's Station, TN

ISBN: 978-1-939946-82-9 (Print)
ISBN: 978-1-939946-83-6 (eBook)

Library of Congress Cataloging-in-Publication Data
Green, Stephanie, 1971–
  Miscarriage : you are not alone / Stephanie Green.
      pages cm
  ISBN 978-1-939946-82-9 — ISBN 978-1-939946-83-6 (ebook)
1. Consolation. 2. Miscarriage—Religious aspects—Christianity.
3. Children—Death—Religious aspects—Christianity.
4. Bereavement—Religious aspects—Christianity. I. Title.
  BV4907.G73 2014
  248.8'66—dc23

                                                    2014026149

Printed in Canada

21 20 19 18 17 16 15 14   1 2 3 4 5

Today I see blood spots and instantly wonder whether something is wrong. Taking a couple of minutes to gain composure, I call my doctor. My doctor directs me to the hospital for testing. Only a few minutes have passed since I arrived at the hospital, but it seems like hours as I wait for answers. I am trying to be hopeful, but deep down I fear the worst.

Finally, they call me back to the ultrasound room. As I watch the screen, my fears become reality and my heart begins to break as I see my precious little baby lifeless, moving only when the ultrasound probe moves him. I wonder, How can this be happening and why is it happening to me?

My doctor prescribed a medicine for me that would induce labor. Twenty-four hours later my lifeless baby was born.

A day later my doctor wants me to have another ultrasound. I wonder what the point is, but they insist on doing it. Nothing could have prepared me for what I was about to see. As I lie on the table my heart is broken while I stare at the screen. What once held a precious life is now just a dark and empty hole. My precious baby I had so many hopes and dreams for is gone. I begin to feel very alone and inadequate. I have so many questions, but where do I go to get answers?

You may be looking at this minibook because the experience described above is one that is similar to your own. Or you might know someone who has experienced a miscarriage and you desire to help her carry the burden.

If you have had a miscarriage, you know firsthand how difficult it can be to work through. You are probably reeling from the whole painful experience, and you need not just physical healing, but emotional and spiritual healing as well. It's common to feel alone as you suffer through painful physical and emotional struggles.

But you have not been left to deal with your suffering alone. You *do* have a loving Father who will help you in the midst of your heartache. As you turn to him with your sadness and pain, you will find that he understands your weakness, your fear, and your sorrow, and he will give you the grace to endure. *And* he will restore your hope. Perhaps you are feeling too weak right now to do much. But take a moment to read this minibook, and let the truth of God's love and his promises fill your heart and mind.

The Aftermath of Your Miscarriage

Start by acknowledging some of the significant suffering you have already faced. With miscarriage there are so many vivid images and physical realities that make it difficult to think about anything other than your current situation. Ultrasounds are wonderful when your baby is healthy and growing. However, seeing an ultrasound picture during your miscarriage creates images in your mind that are constantly replayed and hard to erase. The miscarriage process is also both mentally and physically exhausting. For some there is fear of the unknown, pain, hours or days of waiting, contractions that never seem to end, and bleeding. For others there is surgery (D&C) and recovery. Others may face a combination of the two previous lists. Each story is unique. Each story is special. But each story also shares the same sad theme—there is no baby to take home.

Losing a baby is also difficult emotionally. You have cried so much that you wonder if there could possibly be any tears left, only to find that tears continue to flow easily. Your heart aches over the death of your baby. You wake up hoping your experience was just a bad dream, and when you realize it wasn't, you are faced with another long day.

The long days that follow a miscarriage can be full of so many different emotions. In most instances as soon as a woman finds out she is pregnant, she begins to think about what the next several years are going to look like. She imagines what her baby will look like, picks out a name for him or her, and plans how the days and months following his or her birth will play out. There is an excitement in celebrating this new season of motherhood. The bond between mother and baby is already strong, even after just a few hours of finding out there is a baby in her womb. As you know, the bond increases after each successful week of pregnancy. It increases when you hear the heartbeat for the first time and see your baby moving on an ultrasound. The excitement continues to build until that day when the cramping starts and the bleeding begins. All the dreams you had for yourself and this baby are instantly dashed. The amount of pain and sorrow at that point is indescribable and often unbearable.

Some days you find yourself wondering, *What just happened? How did it happen? Why did it happen?* Other days you may find yourself angry over your circumstances. Angry that it did happen and that it happened to you. Angry because it seems like no one cares as much as you do about the loss of this precious life. Angry that God allowed you to experience the pain and suffering involved in having a miscarriage. You may be angry with friends and family members who are pregnant and enjoying healthy pregnancies. It is normal to feel this way. It is normal to have questions and to struggle with difficulties.

You may have a sense of guilt, thinking that the miscarriage was a result of something you did or didn't do. You may be embarrassed or feel a sense of shame because you were unable to carry this baby to full term. All of these emotions can be the result of your grief and suffering.

During this time it is easy to distance yourself from extended family, friends, and even your husband. You might feel as if you are the only one who understands your suffering and the many thoughts and emotions that follow.

Perhaps you feel alone. There are many reasons for this. Though women often begin planning the next eighteen years the moment they read a positive pregnancy test, they often wait to share their news with others until after the first trimester. When a miscarriage takes place within those first twelve weeks, few people knew that you were pregnant. Therefore very few people, if any, know of your loss and possible need for help and support. That can add to the feeling that you are facing this challenge by yourself.

Another reason you may feel alone is because so few women talk about having miscarriages. In fact, sometimes when other women hear about your miscarriage, they simply approach you with these words: "I have had a miscarriage too." That's all they say! As if knowing that someone else has experienced a miscarriage is going to help you and provide you with comfort in the midst of such heartache and suffering. As a result, you may have had few opportunities to learn from others how God is the source of comfort in miscarriage.

Sometimes we actually promote our sense of aloneness by not sharing openly because we are embarrassed or feel a sense of shame—as if the miscarriage were our fault. We are used to having a certain amount of control, or at least the illusion of control, over our bodies, and we forget that sin's curse has impacted us physically. But miscarriage is one of many ways death intrudes on us, and we are helpless to stop it.

Or perhaps we've had the sad experience of communicating our loss with someone who didn't know how to respond, with someone who minimized our trial, or worse, with someone who told us to suck it up and get over it. So we shut others out of our lives by keeping our sorrow to ourselves, and experience aching aloneness. Our hearts may be breaking, but we tell everyone we're fine. We want to be comforted, but at times wonder if that is even possible in the midst of such heartache. The challenges of miscarriage encourage us to withdraw, hope time will heal our pain, and settle for short-term comforts.

That's quite a list of challenges! And perhaps you are experiencing struggles that I haven't even mentioned. But let me offer you some encouragement: you do not have to tough this out on your own. Despite how you are feeling, you are not alone in your struggles. God is with you. This truth might not seem like much comfort now, but keep reading to learn about the healing God brings in the midst of your heartache.

God Gives True Comfort

"Blessed be the God and Father of our Lord Jesus Christ, the Father of mercies and God of all comfort, who comforts us in all our affliction so that we will be able to comfort those who are in any affliction with the comfort with which we ourselves are comforted by God" (2 Corinthians 1:3–4).

In this passage Paul the apostle describes God as the "Father of mercies." This may be a challenging concept to grasp, as you may live with folks who would better be described as the "father of annoyances" or the "father of irritation." However, God is nothing like that. He is the Father of mercies. The term *mercy* is more commonly described as compassion or kindness, especially in terms of relieving sorrow. Paul describes God as the Father who is compassionate and kind—the One who can help relieve the sorrow and grief you are currently experiencing. What better place to go!

Paul goes on to say that God is the "God of all comfort." In other words, he is with us when we are hurting. Picture a mother who is taking care of her sick child. She is with him and stays with him, tenderly and lovingly caring for his needs. Just as a sick child can count on the presence of his mother, so can you count on the presence of God, who will tenderly and lovingly comfort you in the darkest of days. He is uniquely qualified and able to provide you with all the comfort and mercy you need. The comfort from people, your husband, or your family and friends is wonderful, but it can't compete with the comfort that the Lord can provide.

When we suffer we instinctively know that we need comfort. You might have noticed that you are doing those things that have brought you a measure of comfort in the past. You may find that spending time at the mall shopping gets your mind off your present circumstances and provides some comfort. Or maybe food is of great comfort to you, and you begin eating even when you are not necessarily hungry. How about exercising? Exercising often helps you focus on something other than your current situation.

There is nothing wrong with shopping, eating, or exercising, but they were never meant to be our source of ultimate comfort. They might provide a temporary escape from the hurt and pain of the present. Over time, however, these temporary fixes will prove insufficient in providing the lasting comfort we so desire. True comfort can only be found in God, the Father of mercies and God of all comfort. He will provide the mercy and grace you need to make it through your pain and suffering.

Mercy and Grace for Your Time of Need

Why is that so? Because only he has plumbed the depths of pain and loss, and therefore understands our sorrow. As the writer of Hebrews tells us,

> For we do not have a high priest who cannot sympathize with our weaknesses, but One who has been tempted in all things as we are, yet without sin. Therefore let us draw near with confidence to the throne of grace, so that we may receive mercy and find grace to help in time of need. (Hebrews 4:15–16)

There are three truths in this passage that are exceedingly powerful as we seek God's comfort in the midst of our suffering.

1. Jesus understands. Although Jesus did not have a miscarriage, notice the words of the text that describe him as "tempted in all things." This means that Jesus endured challenges that have remarkable similarities to all the ones we endure. When Jesus cried, "My God, my God, why have you forsaken me?" from the cross, he expressed anguish over the loss of his relationship with his Father. This cry expresses the depth of his suffering, and it is this suffering that puts Jesus in the best possible position to understand all that you are experiencing.

2. Draw near to Jesus. It is not God's desire for you to live in a world of silence where you suffer alone.

Instead, go to Jesus and ask him for all the grace and help you need. Say this out loud—or write it out in a journal. Tell Jesus about the ways you are suffering—all of your fears, worries, sorrows, and struggles. Remember that through his Spirit, Jesus is always with you. Of course it's comforting when others come alongside and help. However, every other human has their own life with their own responsibilities. Jesus is always there. Jesus can be a help every second of every day. When your husband and/or children leave for the day, Jesus is still there. When you wake up in the middle of the night in tears, Jesus is still there. When you are having one of those "moments" on the freeway, Jesus is still there. Dear friend, Jesus will be there long after this minibook has found its way into the trash or onto the bookshelf where it will inevitably be covered with dust.

There is no one else like Jesus—a friend who completely understands and never leaves. So draw near to him. Treat him as the friend who is near and communicate with him continuously in prayer. Look through the Bible and search for passages about his comfort and love. Ask others how Jesus has comforted them through his Word. Look up the passages that helped them. In all of these ways, draw near to Jesus. As you do, you will find grace and mercy to help in your time of need.

3. *Jesus provides everything you need.* At the moment, handling suffering in a way that honors God and serves others may seem impossible, if it is even on your radar at all. Jesus knows this, and he knows that you are ill-equipped to handle everything coming at

you. Because he has experienced all the temptations that come with suffering and yet was perfectly obedient, not only can he sympathize with your weakness, but he also offers you his help to overcome the challenges you are experiencing.

- *Being fearful.* Miscarriage is often accompanied by fear, which may manifest itself in many ways. These are two that tend to come up most often and run most deeply:
    - "Will I be able to have another child?" This is a common concern that plagues many women after a miscarriage. It is easy to find yourself thinking about the possibility of never being able to get pregnant again and spiraling further into despair. Philippians 4:8 calls you to think on things that are true, honorable, right, pure, lovely, and of good repute. Notice it doesn't say to think on the "what-ifs." Yet how many times do you find your thoughts focused there? It is easy to do, especially when you long to have a baby. How do you put aside fear and focus on truth? By turning your eyes to the One who is perfectly true, honorable, right, pure, lovely, and of good repute. He is the only one who knows the future and will provide for you and walk with you through whatever it holds. When you find your mind wandering down the path

of "what-ifs," remember that you can entrust yourself and your future to the God who cares for you. You can "cast all your anxiety on Him, because He cares for you" (1 Peter 5:7).

~ "My husband will reject me." Practically speaking, this is a hard one. Some men are insensitive to their wife, either because they felt no connection to the child yet or because they are unsure how to help. In other instances, however, you may perceive your husband as rejecting you because he is processing the miscarriage much differently than you. Does this mean he doesn't care about the precious life that died? I would like to suggest that this is often not the case at all. As you communicate with your husband, you will usually find that the hurt and pain are real to him as well. It is true that he didn't have the baby inside him, and he is not dealing with the physical side effects of miscarriage or the constant playbacks of that day, but God created him with emotions too. Remember that this precious child was his as well. Talk to your husband. Ask him how he is doing. Consider his thoughts and feelings toward the loss, and share yours with him.

• *Falling into self-pity.* Self-pity can be described as dwelling on your sorrows. In other words, a "woe is me" attitude. You focus your thoughts and attention on what has happened to you and what has been taken from you, and that focus is entirely self-centered. If there's one person in the Bible who knows what loss is, it's Job. As you read the first chapter of the book of Job, you'll notice that Job was a very wealthy man. He had seven sons, three daughters, thousands of livestock, and many servants. He was described as being the greatest of all the men of the east. Greatness notwithstanding, there was one particular day I am sure Job never forgot. It was the day when all of these possessions were taken from him. His children died, his livestock was stolen, and his servants were killed. If anyone had reason to feel sorry for himself, Job did. However, look at Job's response:

> Then Job arose and tore his robe and shaved his head, and he fell to the ground and worshiped. He said, "Naked I came from my mother's womb, and naked I shall return there. The LORD gave and LORD has taken away. Blessed be the name of the LORD." Through all this Job did not sin nor did he blame God. (Job 1:20–22)

Job responded to this incredible tragedy by worshiping God. Job gives us a picture of someone who enters fully into grief, but does not give way to self-pity. Worshiping God in the face of suffering does not mean you don't feel the pain of loss. Nor does it mean that you don't have questions. (Job certainly had many questions.) It simply means that, like Job, you focus on God's character to carry you through, instead of allowing yourself to be swallowed up by grief.

- *Focusing your life on getting pregnant.* After a miscarriage it is easy to make getting pregnant and having another baby the center of your life. Everything revolves around your menstrual cycle. Intercourse is planned according to that cycle and the day on the calendar. Instead of having the goal of pleasing God by pleasing one another during intimate times, sex becomes a task that is routine and based on a schedule. Then day twenty-eight comes. For the past month you have thought about nothing other than getting pregnant, and you approach this day with great fear and anxiety. Are you going to start your period? It is easy to become consumed by the desire to be pregnant, but God has given you many other responsibilities and blessings. When you allow your desire for a baby to dominate your life, then you have let a good and God-given desire take God's place in your life. You've probably already noticed that this adds an extra burden to your life—anxiety, fear, and even anger if things don't work out as you plan. That's how idolatry always affects us. You might feel trapped now, but there is a way forward. Turn to God, tell him all about what you want and how it is affecting you, and ask him to forgive you for Jesus's sake and help you keep him and his love for you at the center of your life.

* *Being jealous.* Jealousy can be a real challenge as others around you become pregnant, start showing signs of pregnancy, and then deliver healthy babies. It can also occur when someone you know is due with her baby around the same time you were—before you miscarried. It can be easy to justify your negative feelings toward these other women, but you must begin to see your response for what it is. James 3:16 says, "For where jealousy and selfish ambition exist, there is disorder and every evil thing." While it may seem innocuous, jealousy grows and festers, destroying you and your relationships. Ask God to help you love these women and their babies. Ask him to help you "rejoice with those who rejoice" (Romans 12:15), even while you are still grieving. Instead of avoiding others who are expecting, show love to them by taking an honest interest in their pregnancy. Rejoice with them during each stage. This can be difficult to do, but our gracious God can help you as you seek to please him in this way.

Let's admit, the above challenges are very real and can easily become a part of your life after losing a baby. It can be easy to succumb to fear, self-pity, idolatry, and jealousy. When you find yourself in the midst of these challenges, choose to draw near to God. He understands and will provide you with the grace and mercy you need.

Share God's Comfort with Others

You've acknowledged your suffering. You've seen how God provides you with true comfort. You've also seen how God provides you with the mercy and grace to help in your time of need. So now what? As you experience God's comfort and begin to heal, you have an opportunity to comfort others. Second Corinthians 1:3–4 gives responsibility to you as well: since you have been comforted, you are supposed to comfort. One of the best ways for you to live for Jesus is to begin ministering to others in similar situations. You are not their savior—that is Jesus's role alone—but you can be used by the Savior to bring comfort and help.

You may be thinking, *But what would I say? What do I have to offer?* Because you have experienced miscarriage, you have been given an amazing opportunity to invest in the lives of other women who are experiencing heartache from losing a baby. You are in the best position to come alongside and comfort them with the comfort you received from God. So, in those dark and lonely days following a miscarriage, you can listen as a friend shares her story and weep with her when the pain and suffering are still very fresh. You can share how God comforted you; how he helped you in the midst of those challenging days. You can share the challenges you faced and how you worked through them. You are able to answer the personal questions that result from having a miscarriage. And by God's grace you are able to use God's Word to offer the hope, encouragement, and comfort you have received.

Because you have experienced miscarriage, you are also more aware of physical needs that may be present. In each situation always ask what would be most helpful. Every woman has her own way of handling grief. Some welcome as much help as they can get. Others want to get back to their normal routine as quickly as possible. Try to meet each woman where she is and offer the support she wants.

Consider the following specific ways to serve:

- If she has other children, ask her if it would be helpful to take them for a day so she can rest.
- Ask if it would be helpful to take her dinner so she doesn't have to worry about cooking.
- Ask her if it would be helpful to clean her home.
- Ask her if it would be helpful to pick up lunch at her favorite restaurant and eat with her to help break up a long and lonely day.

The opportunities to share your care and concern for her are endless; all you need is a willingness to do so.

Please remember that all of this takes time. As we've already noted, women grieve differently. That means not only how they grieve, but also the length of time they grieve.

Many women are going to follow you in experiencing miscarriage. I encourage you to set your goal to be able both to receive comfort from the Lord and to comfort others with the same comfort you have received. Pray that God will use the challenge of miscarriage in your own life to help others who are experiencing it. Pray that God will give you opportunities to encourage, comfort, and give hope to another woman. You never know how what you share can encourage and help someone who is listening. Take the opportunities God gives you and enjoy the privilege you have to bless someone else.

With Scripture as a reminder, trust confidently in Jesus. Let him guide you as you walk with him, passing the milestones of sadness, loneliness, and not feeling understood. Then you will be leaning on him as you walk through this valley with the One who understands, the One who will never leave you, and the One who comforts you like no other. Proverbs 3:5–6 says, "Trust in the LORD with all your heart and do not lean on your own understanding. In all your ways acknowledge Him, and He will make your paths straight."

Miscarriage gives you an opportunity to trust that God knows what is best and you can trust him even in this sad experience. Isn't it great to know that even in the midst of uncertainty you have a loving God whom you can trust with your life? One woman found that to be the case. Her story follows:

> At the time, I didn't understand why I had to be the one to have a miscarriage. I wished it had never happened to me. I wondered if and how I would ever get over the pain and hurt. Now, years later, I consider it a privilege to have suffered through my miscarriage. This doesn't mean that I would volunteer to experience it again! And it doesn't mean that years later the thoughts and memories have all been erased. In fact, there is still an occasional tear shed, and there are still two dates on the calendar that have not been forgotten, but let me encourage you that it does get easier. By God's grace, you can get through this! As a result of my miscarriage, I have learned so much about who God is. And now I have the opportunity to share firsthand with others who have also suffered through a miscarriage. I never thought I would say this, but I do count it a privilege to be chosen as one who can have a voice in the lives of so many others by directing them to the Father of mercy and of all comfort, by directing them to his Word and by comforting them with the comfort I have received.

I hope the above quote encourages you that you are not alone in your miscarriage, and that God will help you every step of the way. Following are some practical ways to turn to your faithful Savior, Jesus:

1. Commit to memory one of these passages each week for the next several weeks: 1 Corinthians 10:12–13; 2 Corinthians 1:3–4; 5:9; Hebrews 4:15–16.

2. Read Psalm 103. Write out every description of God mentioned in this passage. Reflect on the list you've made, and then spend time in prayer, thanking God for his mercy.

3. Write passages on index cards and review them every day. Suggested passages include Proverbs 3:5–6; Romans 8:28; 2 Corinthians 12:9; Philippians 2:3 and 4:8; and Hebrews 13:5.

4. Communicate honestly with a friend or family member how you are doing. Share the ways God is helping you through your miscarriage, and share the areas you are struggling in and need further growth. Ask them to pray for you and to follow up in a week.

5. Thank God for ten evidences of his goodness in your life right now.

6. Do three loving things for your husband or another woman this week.

Finally, keep in mind the words of 2 Corinthians 12:9: "'My grace is sufficient for you, for power is perfected in weakness.' Most gladly, therefore, I will rather boast about my weaknesses, so that the power of Christ may dwell in me." God's grace is sufficient for you. Draw near to him, and he will draw near to you.

Simple, Quick, Biblical

Advice on Complicated Counseling Issues for Pastors, Counselors, and Individuals

MINIBOOK
CATEGORIES

- Personal Change
- Marriage & Parenting
- Medical & Psychiatric Issues

- Women's Issues
- Singles
- Military

USE YOURSELF | GIVE TO A FRIEND | DISPLAY IN YOUR CHURCH OR MINISTRY

New
Growth
Press

Go to **www.newgrowthpress.com** or call **336.378.7775** to purchase individual minibooks or the entire collection. Durable acrylic display stands are also available to house the minibook collection.